I0017200

Introduction

Digital marketing has transformed the way businesses connect with their audiences, and Meta's platforms—Facebook, Instagram, and WhatsApp—are at the forefront of this revolution. With billions of active users worldwide, these platforms offer unparalleled opportunities for brands to build awareness, drive engagement, and boost sales. However, navigating the intricacies of Meta's advertising ecosystem can be daunting for beginners. This book is here to simplify that journey.

Whether you're a small business owner looking to promote your products or a marketing enthusiast eager to expand your skill set, "Mastering Meta" will guide you step-by-step through the fundamentals of digital marketing and Meta Ads. By the end of this book, you'll not only understand how to leverage these platforms effectively but also feel confident in creating and managing ad campaigns that deliver real results.

Purpose of the book

"Mastering Meta" demystifies Meta's advertising tools, making digital marketing accessible to businesses of all sizes. This book provides a comprehensive guide to leveraging Meta's platforms for effective digital advertising.

Key objectives:

1. Introduce Meta's advertising capabilities and platforms
2. Teach practical skills for creating targeted, optimized campaigns
3. Empower small business owners and marketers to grow their brands through digital advertising

Through clear explanations and real-world examples, the book serves as an essential resource for digital marketing success on Meta platforms.

CHAPTER 1: UNDERSTANDING THE BASICS OF META PLATFORMS

1.1 What Is Meta and Why Does It Matter for Businesses?

Meta is a tech conglomerate that encompasses a suite of social media and communication platforms, notably **Facebook**, **Instagram**, and **WhatsApp**. Here's why it's significant for businesses:

- **Global Reach**: With billions of users, Meta's platforms provide one of the largest audiences for businesses to connect with potential customers worldwide. This reach is particularly beneficial for businesses looking to expand their market outside local boundaries.

- **Integrated Ecosystem**: Meta platforms are interconnected, allowing for cross-platform marketing strategies. For example, a campaign can start on Instagram and continue through a customer's journey on WhatsApp for direct engagement.

- **Advanced Advertising Capabilities**: Meta has developed sophisticated advertising tools that use machine learning to optimize ad delivery for maximum engagement and conversion. This precision targeting means businesses can reach consumers who are most likely to be interested in their offerings.

- **Analytics and Insights**: Through tools like **Facebook Insights, Instagram Insights**, and **WhatsApp Business API**, businesses gain deep insights into customer behaviors, preferences, and engagement metrics, enabling data-driven decision-making.
- **E-commerce Integration**: Features like Instagram Shopping and the ability to link products directly in posts or stories facilitate direct sales from social media platforms, streamlining the buying process for consumers.
- **Community Building**: Platforms like **Facebook Groups** offer businesses the chance to create and nurture communities around their brand, fostering loyalty and direct customer interaction.

1.2 OVERVIEW OF EACH PLATFORM FOR BUSINESS

- **Facebook**:
  - **Pages & Profiles**: Businesses can create a presence that's separate from personal profiles, offering a space for promotions, customer interaction, and content sharing.
  - **Marketplace**: Acts like an online classifieds section where businesses can sell products directly.
  - **Events**: Can be used to promote anything from product launches to sales events, driving both online and offline engagement.
- **Instagram**:
  - **Visual Storytelling**: Its emphasis on high-quality visuals makes it ideal for industries where aesthetics play a significant role in consumer decisions, like fashion, food, and travel.
  - **Influencer Marketing**: Instagram's structure supports collaborations with influencers, providing organic reach through trusted voices.
  - **Stories and Reels**: Offer ephemeral and short-form video content options, respectively, which are popular for quick engagement.
- **WhatsApp**:
  - **Direct Messaging**: Allows for one-on-one or

group communication, which can be used for customer service, direct sales, or sending personalized marketing messages.

- ○ **Business Tools**: The WhatsApp Business app offers features like quick replies, labels for contacts, and a business profile, enhancing operational efficiency.

1.3 Key Differences Between Organic Posts and Paid Ads

- **Organic Posts**:
  - ○ **Algorithm Dependence**: The visibility of organic content is heavily influenced by platform algorithms, which consider factors like engagement rate, user interaction history, and content type.
  - ○ **Community Building**: Focuses on building relationships and loyalty with existing followers, often through consistent, valuable content.
  - ○ **Limited Scale**: Without paid promotion, the growth in reach is slower and depends on organic shares, likes, and comments.
- **Paid Ads**:
  - ○ **Controlled Exposure**: With ads, businesses can dictate exactly who sees their content, when, and how often, providing immediate and potentially vast reach.
  - ○ **Conversion Focus**: Ads can be tailored for specific actions like website visits, product purchases, or app downloads, with clear performance metrics.
  - ○ **Flexible Budgeting**: Businesses can start with small budgets and scale up as they see returns, or target high-value campaigns with larger investments.

Understanding these nuances allows businesses to craft a balanced digital marketing strategy that leverages both organic and paid elements to maximize impact, engagement, and ultimately, ROI.

CHAPTER 2: SETTING THE FOUNDATION FOR SUCCESS

2.1 Creating a Facebook Business Page

A Facebook Business Page is the cornerstone of your social media strategy. It allows your brand to have a professional presence and engage with a wide audience. Here are the steps to set up your page:

1. **Log in to Facebook**: Use your personal account to create a business page.
2. **Navigate to 'Create'**: On the left-hand side of the homepage, click on 'Pages' and then select 'Create New Page.'
3. **Enter Basic Information**: Provide a name, category, and description for your business. Make sure these details align with your brand identity.
4. **Add Visuals**: Upload a profile picture (typically your logo) and a cover photo that represents your brand.
5. **Customize Your Page**: Fill out additional details such as your business hours, contact information, and website link.
6. **Optimize Your About Section**: Write a compelling bio that highlights your value proposition.
7. **Start Posting**: Share your first post to introduce your business and invite your network to like your page.

2.2 Setting Up an Instagram Business Account

Instagram is a visually-driven platform that allows you to showcase your products or services creatively. Follow these steps to set up a business account:

1. **Download the Instagram App**: Available on iOS and Android.
2. **Create an Account**: Sign up using your email or phone number.
3. **Switch to a Business Account**: Go to 'Settings,' then 'Account,' and select 'Switch to Professional Account.' Choose 'Business' as the type.
4. **Complete Your Profile**: Add a profile picture, a catchy bio, and a link to your website. Use keywords to make your profile searchable.
5. **Connect to Facebook**: Link your Instagram account to your Facebook Business Page for seamless content sharing.
6. **Start Posting**: Share high-quality images, videos, and stories to engage your audience.

2.3 Establishing Your WhatsApp Business Presence

WhatsApp Business is a direct and personal way to communicate with your customers. Here's how to set it up:

1. **Download WhatsApp Business**: Available for free on app stores.
2. **Register Your Business**: Use your business phone number to create an account.
3. **Create a Business Profile**: Fill in your business name, description, address, email, and website.
4. **Set Up Automated Messages**: Configure greeting messages, quick replies, and away messages to enhance customer experience.
5. **Organize Contacts**: Use labels to categorize and manage your customer interactions effectively.

6. **Promote Your WhatsApp**: Add your WhatsApp number to your website, social media profiles, and marketing materials.

2.4 Why a Strong Profile Matters

Your social media profiles are often the first impression potential customers have of your business. A well-crafted profile builds credibility, attracts followers, and drives engagement. Here are key elements to focus on:

- **Professional Visuals**: High-quality profile pictures and cover images create a polished look.
- **Compelling Bios**: Use this space to communicate your unique value proposition and include a call-to-action.
- **Consistent Branding**: Ensure that your tone, colors, and messaging align across all platforms.
- **Updated Information**: Keep your contact details, business hours, and website links accurate.
- **Engaging Content**: Regularly post content that resonates with your audience to keep them interested.

Setting up these foundational elements will set the stage for your business's success on social media.

CHAPTER 3: UNDERSTANDING THE BASICS OF META PLATFORMS

1.1 What Is Meta and Why Does It Matter for Businesses?

Meta stands at the forefront of digital interaction, being the parent company to some of the world's most influential social media platforms: **Facebook**, **Instagram**, and **WhatsApp**. Here's why Meta holds such pivotal importance for businesses:

- **Unprecedented Reach**: With billions of users engaging daily, Meta's platforms offer a global stage for businesses to showcase their products or services. This reach transcends geographical boundaries, enabling even small businesses to tap into international markets.

- **Integrated Marketing Opportunities**: Meta's ecosystem allows for seamless cross-platform campaigns. A business can initiate customer interaction on Instagram, continue it on WhatsApp for personalized service, or leverage the community aspect of **Facebook Groups** for deeper engagement.

- **Sophisticated Advertising Tools**: Meta provides advertisers with tools that use advanced algorithms to optimize ad performance. This means businesses can target ads with high precision to demographics, interests, behaviors, and more, ensuring marketing dollars are spent effectively.

- **Data-Driven Insights**: Platforms under Meta offer detailed analytics, allowing businesses to track user engagement, campaign performance, and consumer behavior. This data is invaluable for refining marketing strategies and understanding customer needs.
- **E-commerce Synergy**: Features like Instagram Shopping provide direct links from social media to e-commerce, shortening the sales funnel and enhancing user experience from discovery to purchase.
- **Community and Loyalty**: The ability to create and manage communities on platforms like **Facebook** helps businesses build loyalty, gather feedback, and keep their audience engaged over time.

1.2 Overview of Each Platform for Business

- **Facebook**:
  - **Pages**: A dedicated space for businesses to share content, interact with customers, and run promotions.
  - **Marketplace**: A go-to place for selling products directly, especially useful for local businesses or those with a tangible product line.
  - **Events**: Businesses can advertise and manage events, driving both online interactions and physical footfall.
- **Instagram**:
  - **Visual Engagement**: Perfect for brands where visual appeal is key. The platform allows for storytelling through images, videos, and interactive features like Stories and Reels.
  - **Shopping Experience**: Instagram has integrated shopping features that allow users to buy products directly from posts or stories, enhancing the user journey from browsing to buying.
  - **Influencer Partnerships**: Leveraging influencers can amplify reach and trust among potential customers.
- **WhatsApp**:

- o   **Personalized Interaction**: Offers a channel for direct, personal communication with customers, which is ideal for customer support, sales inquiries, or sending updates.
- o   **Business App**: Provides businesses with tools to manage customer conversations at scale, including automated messages and quick replies.

1.3 Key Differences Between Organic Posts and Paid Ads

- **Organic Posts**:
  - o   **Natural Growth**: These are posts that appear in your audience's feed without payment. They rely on engagement (likes, comments, shares) to increase visibility, which is determined by the platform's algorithms.
  - o   **Community Engagement**: Organic posts are crucial for building a community, sharing brand stories, and maintaining regular interaction with followers.
  - o   **Limitations**: The organic reach can be limited unless content goes viral or is shared extensively.
- **Paid Ads**:
  - o   **Controlled Exposure**: Businesses pay to place their content in front of targeted audiences. This control over who sees your content, when, and how often is a significant advantage over organic reach.
  - o   **Performance Goals**: Ads are designed with specific objectives in mind, such as driving sales, increasing website traffic, or collecting leads. They come with performance metrics for ROI analysis.
  - o   **Flexibility**: You can set your budget, adjust it based on performance, and choose from various ad formats to suit your campaign's needs.

By understanding these foundational elements of Meta's platforms, businesses can strategically plan their digital marketing to leverage both organic growth and paid advertising to their fullest potential. This chapter lays the groundwork for mastering the art of digital marketing within Meta's expansive digital universe.

CHAPTER 4: CREATING COMPELLING CONTENT

Creating content that captivates your audience is at the heart of a successful social media strategy. In this chapter, we'll dive deep into the methods and techniques for producing posts that stand out on Facebook and Instagram, ensuring they resonate with your target audience and drive engagement.

4.1 Best Practices for Posts on Facebook and Instagram

To succeed on Facebook and Instagram, it's essential to tailor your posts to the unique characteristics of each platform while maintaining a consistent brand voice. Here are some best practices:

1. Understand the Audience:

- Research the demographics and behavior of your followers on each platform.
- Use analytics tools like Meta's Insights to determine when your audience is most active.

2. Optimize for Each Platform:

- Facebook: Longer captions and posts with links, videos, or images tend to perform well.
- Instagram: Prioritize high-quality visuals and concise, engaging captions.

3. Consistency is Key:

- Establish a posting schedule that aligns with audience activity.
- Use a content calendar to maintain a steady flow of posts.

4. Encourage Engagement:

- Pose questions or create polls to spark conversation.
- Respond to comments and messages promptly to build community.

5. Test and Adapt:

- Experiment with different content formats and track their performance.
- Refine your strategy based on what resonates most with your audience.

4.2 Choosing High-Quality Visuals and Videos

Visual content is the backbone of Facebook and Instagram. High-quality visuals not only grab attention but also communicate professionalism and trustworthiness. Follow these tips to ensure your visuals stand out:

1. Prioritize Quality:

- Use high-resolution images and videos that are well-lit and properly framed.
- Avoid over-editing or using filters that distort the original content.

2. Align with Your Brand Identity:

- Use consistent colors, fonts, and styles to ensure your visuals reflect your brand.
- Incorporate your logo subtly in videos or images for brand recall.

3. Focus on Storytelling:

- Create visuals that evoke emotion or tell a story.
- Use before-and-after images, behind-the-scenes footage, or customer testimonials to make your content relatable.

4. Use Tools and Resources:

- Leverage design platforms like Canva or Adobe Express for creating professional visuals.
- Opt for stock photo sites if you lack original content but customize them to align with your brand.

5. Optimize for Mobile:

- Ensure images and videos are cropped appropriately for vertical viewing.
- Use captions in videos to make them accessible even without sound.

4.3 Writing Engaging Captions and Call-to-Actions

Captions are your opportunity to add context, personality, and a compelling reason for your audience to engage with your post. Crafting the right message can significantly enhance the impact of your content.

1. Start Strong:

- The first sentence should grab attention, as it's what users see before clicking "More."
- Use humor, a surprising fact, or an emotional hook.

2. Speak Directly to Your Audience:

- Write in a conversational tone that matches your audience's preferences.
- Use "you" to make the caption feel personal.

3. Be Concise Yet Impactful:

- Keep your captions short when possible, but don't shy away from longer captions if you're sharing a story.

- Use line breaks and emojis to improve readability.

4. Include a Clear Call-to-Action (CTA):

- Direct your audience to take action, whether it's "Click the link in bio," "Tag a friend," or "Share your thoughts below."
- Position your CTA at the end of your caption for emphasis.

5. Experiment with Formats:

- Try lists, questions, or bullet points to make your captions more engaging.
- Use hashtags strategically to improve discoverability.

4.4 Leveraging Stories, Reels, and Live Videos

Stories, Reels, and Live Videos offer unique ways to engage with your audience. They provide an opportunity to showcase authenticity, creativity, and real-time interactions.

1. Stories:

- Post regularly to stay visible at the top of your followers' feeds.
- Use interactive stickers like polls, quizzes, and sliders to encourage engagement.
- Share behind-the-scenes content, quick updates, or user-generated content to keep your stories fresh.

2. Reels:

- Create short, entertaining, or educational videos tailored to trending formats.
- Use music, text overlays, and transitions to make your Reels visually dynamic.
- Keep them under 30 seconds for better completion rates.

3. Live Videos:

- Schedule and promote your live sessions in advance to maximize attendance.
- Interact with viewers by responding to comments and

answering questions in real-time.
- Use Live for product launches, Q&A sessions, or collaborations with influencers.

By incorporating these practices into your social media strategy, you'll be equipped to create compelling content that not only engages your audience but also drives meaningful results.

CHAPTER 5: GETTING STARTED WITH BOOSTING POSTS

5.1 What Is a Boosted Post?

A boosted post is a powerful tool that transforms your regular organic social media content into a paid advertisement. Found primarily on platforms like Facebook and Instagram, this feature is an efficient way to extend the reach of your posts without the complexities of setting up a full advertising campaign. Here are the essential aspects of boosted posts:

- **Visibility:** Boosting enables your post to appear in the feeds of users who match your targeting criteria but may not already follow you. This expanded reach increases the likelihood of engaging new audiences.
- **Simplicity:** Unlike the detailed setup required for traditional ads, boosting a post is straightforward. Simply select a post you've already published, define your target audience, allocate a budget, set the duration, and let the platform's algorithm handle the rest.
- **Engagement Focus:** Boosting is particularly useful for driving key engagement metrics such as likes, comments, shares, and clicks. It's most effective when used to amplify posts that are already performing well organically.
- **Sponsored Label:** Once boosted, your post will carry a "Sponsored" label, indicating to users that it is a

paid promotion. This transparency fosters trust while still achieving your promotional goals.

Boosted posts are an excellent entry point for businesses new to paid social media advertising, offering simplicity and effectiveness with minimal effort.

5.2 How to Boost a Post on Facebook

Boosting a post on Facebook is a simple yet strategic process. Follow these steps to ensure your promotion reaches the right audience:

1. **Choose Your Post:**
   o   Navigate to your Facebook Page and select a post to boost. Ideal candidates are posts with high organic engagement, as they are more likely to perform well when promoted. This could include photos, videos, links, or status updates.
2. **Click 'Boost Post':**
   o   Under the selected post, locate the 'Boost Post' button. Clicking this will open the boost options, where you can customize your promotion settings.
3. **Set Your Objective:**
   o   Choose from available objectives, such as increasing page likes, driving website visits, or boosting post engagement. Your chosen goal will guide the platform in optimizing your ad's delivery.
4. **Define Your Audience:**
   o   **Location:** Specify geographic areas to target.
   o   **Demographics:** Select age and gender preferences.
   o   **Interests:** Identify the hobbies, behaviors, or activities your target audience might engage in.
   o   **Automatic vs. Custom:** Opt for Facebook's automatic audience selection based on your existing followers or manually define a custom audience.
5. **Set Your Budget and Duration:**

o   Decide how much to spend and how long to run the promotion. Budgets can range from a few dollars to more significant amounts, depending on your goals. Durations can be as short as a day or extend over weeks.

6. **Payment:**
o   Ensure your payment details are updated in the Ads Manager or within the boost interface.

7. **Review and Activate:**
o   Preview your boosted post to verify its appearance and settings. Once satisfied, click 'Boost' to activate the promotion.

5.3 Tips for Boosting Instagram Posts

Boosting posts on Instagram follows a similar approach to Facebook but emphasizes visuals and platform-specific nuances. Here's how to make the most of your Instagram boosts:

1. **Choose High-Performance Content:**
o   Select posts with strong organic engagement. Content that resonates with your existing audience is more likely to succeed when promoted.

2. **Prioritize Visual Quality:**
o   Instagram is a visual-first platform, so use high-quality images or videos that align with your brand's aesthetic and catch the viewer's eye.

3. **Include a Clear Call-to-Action (CTA):**
o   Craft compelling captions with clear CTAs, such as "Shop Now," "Learn More," or "Message Us." A strong CTA can guide users toward your desired outcome, whether it's a website visit or a direct interaction.

4. **Optimize Audience Targeting:**
o   Use Instagram's targeting options to refine your audience by interests, behaviors, and demographics. Tailor your audience to reflect the ideal customer for your product or service.

5. **Monitor Performance:**
   o   Regularly check metrics like reach, engagement, and conversions. If a boosted post underperforms, stop it early and reallocate your budget to more effective content.

6. **Experiment with Stories:**
   o   Instagram Stories are an excellent format for boosting time-sensitive promotions or driving quick actions, like visiting a website or exploring a product. Stories provide an immersive, full-screen experience that captures attention.

5.4 When to Boost Posts vs. Create Dedicated Ads

Deciding whether to boost a post or create a dedicated ad campaign depends on your objectives, resources, and desired level of control. Here's a breakdown of when to choose each approach:

- **Speed and Simplicity:**
  o   Boosting is ideal for quickly amplifying content without extensive planning. It's perfect for time-sensitive promotions or for testing the potential of a high-performing organic post.
- **Control and Customization:**
  o   Dedicated ads, created through Ads Manager, offer advanced options such as A/B testing, detailed audience segmentation, and various ad formats (e.g., carousel, video, or collection ads). Use this option for comprehensive marketing strategies.
- **Budget Flexibility:**
  o   Boosted posts are accessible for smaller budgets, making them a great choice for businesses with limited advertising funds. For larger campaigns or when optimizing spend over time, dedicated ads provide greater flexibility and insights.
- **Goals and Metrics:**
  o   Boosting is best suited for short-term engagement,

such as promoting an event or highlighting a special offer. Dedicated ads are more effective for long-term goals like lead generation, brand awareness, or driving conversions.

- **Creative Needs:**
  - If your campaign requires customized visuals, landing pages, or specific messaging tailored to multiple audiences, a dedicated ad setup is necessary.

By understanding the strengths and limitations of both options, you can strategically enhance your social media presence while aligning with your business goals.

Boosting posts is a powerful and accessible way to increase visibility and engagement. By mastering this feature and knowing when to opt for dedicated ads, you can optimize your social media advertising efforts to achieve both short-term and long-term success.

CHAPTER 6: CRAFTING ADS WITH META TOOLS

6.1 Introduction to Meta Ads Manager

Meta Ads Manager is more than just a tool; it's a comprehensive advertising suite that empowers businesses to execute sophisticated marketing strategies across multiple platforms including **Facebook**, **Instagram**, **Messenger**, and the **Audience Network**. This platform is engineered to cater to marketers at any level of expertise, offering a blend of simplicity for beginners and depth for seasoned advertisers. Here's how:

- **Campaign Structure**: Ads Manager organizes your advertising efforts into a clear hierarchy - campaigns, ad sets, and ads. This structure helps in managing and tracking different objectives and strategies systematically.

- **Custom Audiences**: With this feature, you can target your ads with surgical precision, based on a plethora of criteria like demographics, interests, behaviors, or even based on interactions with your website or app. This level of customization ensures that your message reaches only the most relevant audience.

- **Detailed Reporting**: Real-time data on metrics like reach, impressions, engagement, click-through rates, and conversions allow you to understand what's working and what isn't. This insight is crucial for optimizing campaigns for better performance.

- **A/B Testing**: Test different elements of your ads

(like images, headlines, call-to-actions) against each other to see which combination yields the best results. This empirical approach to advertising ensures continuous improvement in ad performance.

- **Flexibility and Control**: Whether you're aiming for broad awareness or specific conversions, Ads Manager provides the controls to tweak every aspect of your ad campaign, from budget allocation to ad placement.

This tool is pivotal for achieving a high ROI by ensuring that your advertising dollars are spent wisely and effectively.

6.2 Types of Ads You Can Create
Meta's advertising ecosystem supports a variety of ad formats, each designed to cater to different marketing objectives:

1. **Carousel Ads**:
   o **Functionality**: Allows you to display multiple images or videos within one ad, each with its own link and call-to-action.
   o **Use Cases**: Excellent for showing off product lines, step-by-step guides, or telling a narrative through multiple visuals.
2. **Video Ads**:
   o **Engagement**: Videos capture and retain user attention much better than static images, making them perfect for storytelling or product demos.
   o **Placement**: Can be used in feeds, stories, Reels, or as video ads in the Audience Network.
3. **Image Ads**:
   o **Simplicity**: A single image with text can communicate your message clearly and effectively.
   o **Versatility**: Suitable for any stage of the marketing funnel, from awareness to conversion.
4. **Collection Ads**:
   o **Interactive**: Combines a video or image with a product catalog, allowing users to browse products directly from the ad.
   o **E-Commerce**: Streamlines the shopping experience by

bringing the store to the user's feed.

5. **Instant Experience Ads**:

o   **Immersive**: Offers a full-screen, vertical experience that can include images, videos, and interactive elements.

o   **Storytelling**: Ideal for providing a detailed look at products or services, enhancing user engagement.

6. **Lead Ads**:

o   **Conversion Focused**: Designed to collect information from users with minimal effort, using pre-filled forms.

o   **Efficiency**: Reduces friction in the lead generation process, making it easier to gather contact details or survey responses.

Each ad type is not just a format but a strategy tailored to engage users in different ways, driving various business outcomes.

6.3 Step-by-Step Guide to Creating an Ad Campaign

Creating an ad campaign in Ads Manager involves several steps, each allowing you to fine-tune your approach:

Step 1: Access Ads Manager

- Log into your Meta Business Suite.
- Click on "Ads Manager" from the "Advertise" section.

Step 2: Choose a Campaign Objective

- Decide what you want to achieve. Options include raising awareness, increasing traffic, boosting engagement, gathering leads, or driving conversions.
- Your choice here will dictate how Meta optimizes your ad delivery.

Step 3: Define Your Audience

- **Location**: Target by country, region, or even zip codes.
- **Demographics**: Age, gender, language, education, job titles, etc.
- **Interests**: Leverage user interests, behaviors, and connections to tailor your audience.

Step 4: Set Your Budget and Schedule

- **Budget**: Choose a daily or lifetime budget. Daily budget ensures consistent spending, while lifetime is ideal for campaigns with a definite end date.

- **Schedule**: Specify when your ads will run, including start and end dates, or use scheduling for specific times of the day or week.

Step 5: Design Your Ad
- **Media**: Upload your visuals, ensuring they comply with Meta's specs for each ad type.
- **Text**: Write headlines, descriptions, and calls-to-action that resonate with your audience.
- **CTA**: Select a call-to-action that aligns with your objective, like "Shop Now," "Learn More," or "Sign Up."

Step 6: Review and Publish
- Review your setup for accuracy in targeting, budget, and creative elements.
- Once satisfied, click "Publish" to launch your campaign.

6.4 Using Facebook Stock Images and Creative Tools
Meta provides an arsenal of creative resources to help you produce ads that stand out:

- **Using Facebook Stock Images**:
  - Access high-quality, royalty-free images directly within Ads Manager.
  - Search by keyword to find images that fit your ad's theme or product.
- **Creative Tools**:
  - **Ad Mockup Tools**: See previews of your ads across different devices and placements.
  - **Text Overlay Checker**: Ensure your ad's visual balance by checking if text covers too much of the image.
  - **Video Creation Kit**: Even if you're not a video expert, these templates let you produce professional videos with your brand's touch.
  - **Sound Collection**: Add the right audio to your videos to enhance the message or mood.

These resources democratize high-end ad creation, allowing businesses of all sizes to produce visually appealing and effective ads without the need for external creative services.

By mastering these tools within Meta Ads Manager, you not only streamline your advertising process but also significantly enhance the potential impact of your campaigns. Whether you're just starting or looking to refine your approach, the capabilities of Ads Manager are there to help you achieve your marketing objectives with precision and creativity.

CHAPTER 7: BUDGETING AND AD PERFORMANCE

7.1 How Ad Budgets Work (Daily vs. Lifetime Budgets)

Allocating your advertising budget effectively is crucial to running successful campaigns on Meta platforms. Understanding the two primary budget types—daily and lifetime—can help you align your spending with your campaign objectives.

Daily Budgets

- **Definition:** A daily budget sets the maximum amount you're willing to spend each day on your ad campaign.
- **Mechanism:** Meta's system strives to distribute your spending evenly throughout the day. However, fluctuations may occur based on ad demand and performance. For example, on days when your ad is performing exceptionally well, Meta may spend slightly more than your daily budget but will compensate by spending less on other days, ensuring the average daily spend aligns with your budget.
- **Flexibility:** This budget type provides flexibility and control over daily expenditures, making it easier to monitor and adjust campaigns as needed.
- **Use Case:** Ideal for ongoing campaigns where consistent visibility is key. This approach suits businesses that aim for steady engagement without committing to a large, upfront sum.

Lifetime Budgets

- **Definition:** A lifetime budget is the total amount you allocate for an ad campaign over its entire duration.
- **Mechanism:** Meta optimizes your budget allocation by predicting periods of higher engagement. This allows your ad to achieve better results by spending more when performance is expected to peak.
- **Control:** You have more control over total spending, ensuring the budget remains within set limits even if engagement surges.
- **Use Case:** Best suited for campaigns with specific time frames or objectives, such as product launches, seasonal sales, or event promotions. It's particularly useful for ensuring that your budget isn't exhausted prematurely during high-traffic periods.

Both budgeting methods require strategic consideration. Depending on campaign objectives and audience behavior, you can decide which approach better suits your marketing goals.

7.2 Setting a Budget for Your Campaigns

Setting an ad budget isn't merely about choosing an amount; it involves strategic allocation to maximize impact. Here's how to approach it:

1. **Determine Your Goals**
   o Align your budget with specific campaign objectives. For instance, campaigns focused on brand awareness might allocate more funds to reach and impressions, while conversion campaigns may focus on cost per acquisition (CPA).
2. **Research and Benchmark**
   o Understand industry benchmarks for key metrics like cost-per-click (CPC) and cost-per-thousand-impressions (CPM). These figures can serve as a reference point for setting realistic budgets.

3. **Start Small, Scale Smart**

o   For new advertisers, begin with a modest budget to test various ad sets and gather performance insights. Once you identify high-performing ads, allocate additional budget to scale them up.

4. **Consider the Sales Funnel**

o   Allocate resources based on your target audience's position in the sales funnel. For example, awareness campaigns at the top of the funnel may require a larger budget to capture attention, while retargeting campaigns at the bottom may need less but yield higher conversions.

5. **Seasonal Adjustments**

o   Increase budgets during peak seasons or around special events when engagement and purchasing behavior are expected to rise. For example, holidays or promotional events may warrant higher spending to capture more audience attention.

6. **Test and Learn**

o   Use A/B testing to experiment with different ad creatives, formats, and targeting strategies. Allocate portions of your budget to these tests and refine your approach based on the results.

7. **Competitive Analysis**

o   Monitor competitors' advertising strategies, including their frequency and creativity. If they're outspending or outpacing you, consider adjusting your budget to maintain competitive visibility.

7.3 Understanding Bidding and Auctions

Meta uses an auction-based system to determine which ads are displayed to users. Understanding this system can help you optimize your bids and ad performance.

Bidding Strategies

- **Lowest Cost (Automatic Bidding):** Meta automatically sets bids to maximize results within your budget.

- **Target Cost:** You specify a desired cost per action (CPA), and Meta adjusts bids to meet this target.
- **Bid Cap:** You set a maximum bid for actions, providing greater control over costs but potentially limiting ad reach.
- **Cost Cap:** Similar to Target Cost but ensures you won't pay more than the specified maximum per action.

Ad Auction Dynamics

1. **Ad Quality and Relevance:** High-quality ads that resonate with users can win auctions even with lower bids.
2. **Estimated Action Rates:** Ads with higher predicted engagement rates tend to win auctions at lower costs.
3. **User Value:** Meta evaluates the potential lifetime value of users engaging with your ad, influencing its delivery.

Auction Process When a user loads their feed, Meta conducts a real-time auction for available ad slots. It evaluates all eligible ads based on their bids, quality scores, and relevance to the user's context. The winning ad is the one that delivers the highest value to the user—not necessarily the one with the highest bid.

Understanding this process enables advertisers to bid strategically, focusing on ad quality and relevance rather than just increasing bid amounts.

7.4 Tracking Key Metrics to Measure Success

Tracking and analyzing key performance metrics is essential for evaluating campaign success and optimizing future efforts. Here are the most important metrics to monitor:

- **Impressions:** The total number of times your ad was displayed. Useful for gauging visibility in awareness campaigns.
- **Reach:** The number of unique users who saw your ad, indicating the breadth of your campaign's exposure.

- **Click-Through Rate (CTR):** The percentage of impressions that resulted in clicks. High CTRs indicate strong ad relevance and engagement.
- **Conversion Rate:** The percentage of clicks that led to desired actions, such as purchases or sign-ups. This metric directly measures campaign effectiveness.
- **Cost Per Click (CPC):** The amount spent for each click. Lower CPCs are preferable but should be evaluated alongside conversion quality.
- **Cost Per Acquisition (CPA):** The cost of acquiring a customer or lead. Essential for assessing return on investment (ROI).
- **Return on Ad Spend (ROAS):** Revenue generated per dollar spent on ads. A high ROAS indicates a profitable campaign.
- **Engagement Rate:** Measures likes, shares, and comments, reflecting how well your content resonates with the audience.
- **Frequency:** The average number of times a user sees your ad. High frequency can lead to ad fatigue and reduced effectiveness.
- **Quality Ranking:** Meta's assessment of your ad's quality compared to competitors in the same auction.

Best Practices for Tracking Metrics:

- **Implement Tracking Pixels:** Install Meta Pixel on your website to accurately track conversions and user actions.
- **Leverage Analytics Tools:** Use Meta Insights along with third-party tools to analyze user behavior post-click.
- **Conduct A/B Testing:** Test various ad elements to identify what resonates most with your audience and optimize accordingly.

By consistently monitoring these metrics, you can refine your advertising strategies, allocate budgets effectively, and ensure your campaigns deliver measurable results aligned with your business objectives.

CHAPTER 8: TARGETING THE RIGHT AUDIENCE

Effective targeting is the cornerstone of a successful marketing campaign. This chapter will guide you through the tools and techniques necessary to pinpoint your ideal audience, optimize your reach, and maximize your return on investment.

8.1 Automatic vs. Custom Audiences

Platforms like Meta Ads Manager and Google Ads offer automatic audience targeting as a quick, beginner-friendly option. These tools use machine learning to identify potential customers based on your campaign goals. While convenient, automatic audiences may not always align perfectly with your brand's niche.

Custom audiences, on the other hand, allow for more precision. By uploading customer data, such as email lists or website visitor activity, you can directly target individuals who have already shown interest in your business. This approach provides higher relevance and conversion rates but requires more effort in data collection and segmentation.

Key takeaway: Use automatic audiences for initial testing and broad campaigns. Shift to custom audiences as you gather data and refine your strategy.

8.2 Using Demographics, Interests, and Behaviors

Understanding your audience's demographics, interests, and

behaviors is vital. These factors help you create profiles that align with your ideal customer:

- **Demographics:** Age, gender, location, language, and income levels.
- **Interests:** Hobbies, favorite brands, or lifestyle choices.
- **Behaviors:** Purchase habits, device usage, and online activity.

For example, if you're marketing eco-friendly skincare products, you might target:

- Women aged 25-45 in urban areas.
- Interests in sustainable living, beauty tips, and wellness blogs.
- Behaviors like frequent online shopping or engagement with beauty-related content.

Most advertising platforms provide tools to layer these attributes, ensuring your ads reach the right people with the right message.

8.3 Retargeting People Who Interact with Your Content

Retargeting is a powerful strategy to re-engage users who have already interacted with your content but haven't converted yet. Here's how it works:

- **Website Visitors:** Use tracking pixels to retarget users who visit specific pages, like a product or pricing page.
- **Engagements on Social Media:** Target users who like, comment, or share your posts.
- **Video Viewers:** Focus on people who watch a significant portion of your video ads.

For example, if someone browses a product page but doesn't complete a purchase, you can serve them an ad offering a discount or highlighting the product's unique benefits. Retargeting nurtures warm leads and increases conversion rates.

8.4 Creating Lookalike Audiences to Expand Your Reach

Lookalike audiences help you scale your campaigns by finding new people who resemble your existing customers. To create these audiences:

1. **Define Your Source Audience:** Use data from high-value customers, such as email lists or pixel data.
2. **Set Geographic Parameters:** Choose regions where you want your ads displayed.
3. **Adjust Similarity Levels:** Most platforms let you choose between small, highly similar audiences or larger, less precise ones. A smaller audience offers higher relevance, while a larger one increases reach.

For instance, if your source audience comprises loyal customers who frequently purchase fitness apparel, a lookalike audience could target individuals with similar interests and buying patterns. This strategy helps expand your market efficiently while maintaining relevance.

CHAPTER 9: SCALING YOUR EFFORTS WITH AUTOMATION

9.1 How Automated Ads Work

Automation in advertising, particularly on Meta's platforms, transforms how businesses manage their ad campaigns by leveraging technology to make data-driven decisions. Here's an in-depth look at how automated ads function:

- **Machine Learning**: At the core, automated ads use machine learning algorithms to analyze vast amounts of data. These algorithms predict which ads will perform best with which audiences, at what times, and in which contexts.
- **Dynamic Optimization**: Once you set your parameters, the system automatically adjusts bids, placements, and even creative elements like headlines or images to optimize for your chosen objectives. For example, if one ad variant is performing well, the system might allocate more budget to it or show it more frequently.
- **Audience Expansion**: Automation can identify and target new audiences that share characteristics with your best-performing segments, thus expanding your reach without additional manual work.
- **Budget Management**: Automated systems manage your budget more efficiently, often achieving better results with the same or even less spend by focusing on high-performing ads and times.
- **Creative Rotation**: Meta's automation can rotate through different creatives to prevent ad fatigue, ensuring that your

audience doesn't see the same ad repeatedly, which might decrease engagement.

- **Responsive Ads**: With automated ads, you can create multiple variations of headlines, descriptions, and images, and the system will test these to find the best combination for your audience.

9.2 Setting Goals for Automated Campaigns

When you decide to automate your advertising efforts, setting clear, measurable goals is crucial:

- **Objective Clarity**: Define what success looks like - is it more website visits, app installs, lead generation, or sales? The objective you choose will guide how the automation algorithms work.
- **SMART Goals**: Ensure your goals are Specific, Measurable, Achievable, Relevant, and Time-bound. For instance, "Increase app downloads by 20% in the next quarter" is a SMART goal.
- **Budget Considerations**: Set budgets according to your goals. Automation can be very effective but requires a sufficient budget to learn and optimize over time.
- **Performance Metrics**: Decide which metrics will indicate success. For conversion-heavy campaigns, this might be CPA (Cost Per Acquisition) or ROAS (Return On Ad Spend); for engagement campaigns, it could be engagement rate or CTR (Click-Through Rate).
- **Audience Goals**: If part of your goal is to reach new audiences, consider setting up automated lookalike audiences or using interest-based targeting that evolves with data.
- **Testing Goals**: Automation allows for A/B testing at scale. Goals here might include finding the best creative elements or understanding which audience segments convert the best.

9.3 Reviewing and Adjusting Automated Ads

Even with automation, regular review and adjustment are key to long-term success:

- **Performance Monitoring**: Use Meta's analytics to track key performance indicators (KPIs) regularly. Look for trends, spikes, or drops in performance that might indicate a need for

adjustment.
- **Ad Fatigue**: Monitor frequency and engagement. If your ads are showing too often to the same people, consider refreshing your creatives or adjusting your audience targeting.
- **A/B Testing Insights**: Regularly review the results of any A/B tests to understand which elements of your ads are most effective, then adjust your automated settings or creatives accordingly.
- **Budget Reallocation**: If certain ads or campaigns are underperforming, the system might not reallocate budget efficiently. Manual intervention might be needed to shift funds towards better-performing ads.
- **Seasonal Adjustments**: Automatically adjust your bids or budgets for seasonal trends or events that could impact your campaign's performance.
- **Feedback Loop**: Use customer feedback or conversion data to refine your targeting or messaging, even if the system is automated.

9.4 Combining Automation with Manual Optimization

While automation is powerful, combining it with human oversight can yield the best results:

- **Creative Direction**: Humans are better at crafting the initial creative strategy. Use automation to test variations but set the tone and messaging manually.
- **Strategic Oversight**: Regularly review automated strategies against business goals. Automation might optimize for efficiency, but you might need to manually adjust for strategic shifts like new product launches or market changes.
- **Data Interpretation**: Automation provides data, but human insight is needed to interpret it in the context of broader business strategies or external factors.
- **Custom Audiences**: While automation can expand audiences, manually creating custom audiences from high-value customer data can lead to more personalized and effective campaigns.
- **Error Checking**: Automated systems can occasionally go off track or misinterpret data. Manual checks can catch these anomalies.

- **Responsive Marketing**: For time-sensitive promotions or responses to market changes, manual adjustments ensure your campaign can react quickly, something automation might not do without specific instructions.
- **Balancing Scale and Precision**: Use automation for scaling and broad strategies, but manually fine-tune for precision in targeting, especially for niche markets or complex buyer journeys.

By understanding how to effectively integrate automation into your advertising strategy, you can scale your efforts with efficiency while still maintaining the personal touch and strategic oversight that can make all the difference in a crowded digital marketplace. This chapter emphasizes that while technology can handle much of the heavy lifting, the human element in marketing remains indispensable for nuanced, successful campaigns.

Targeting the right audience is an ongoing process of testing and refining. Start broad with automatic audiences, then narrow your focus using custom audiences, demographic insights, retargeting strategies, and lookalike audiences. By leveraging these tools effectively, you can ensure your message reaches the right people, at the right time, with the right offer.

CHAPTER 10: ADVANCED STRATEGIES AND BEST PRACTICES

10.1 A/B Testing Ads to Find What Works Best

A/B testing, also known as split testing, is a powerful method to identify what resonates most with your audience. By creating two or more versions of an ad with one variable changed—such as the headline, image, call-to-action, or audience targeting—you can measure which version performs better based on predefined metrics like click-through rate (CTR), conversions, or engagement.

Steps to Conduct Effective A/B Testing:

1. **Define Your Goal:** Decide what you're testing for, whether it's higher clicks, lower cost per acquisition, or increased engagement.
2. **Identify a Single Variable:** Test only one element at a time to ensure clear results. For example, compare two different headlines while keeping all other factors constant.
3. **Set a Sufficient Budget and Duration:** Ensure your test runs long enough and reaches enough people to produce statistically significant results.
4. **Analyze the Results:** Use analytics tools to identify the winning ad. Apply the insights gained to refine future

campaigns.

10.2 CREATING CAMPAIGNS FOR SEASONAL AND TRENDING MOMENTS

Seasonal events and trending topics present unique opportunities to capture attention and drive engagement. Effective campaigns align with moments your audience cares about, such as holidays, sports events, or viral trends.

Best Practices for Seasonal Campaigns:

- **Plan Ahead:** Identify key dates relevant to your industry and audience, such as Black Friday or Valentine's Day. Develop creative assets and schedules well in advance.
- **Leverage Emotional Appeal:** Tailor your messaging to evoke emotions tied to the season, such as gratitude during Thanksgiving or excitement during the World Cup.
- **Use Limited-Time Offers:** Create urgency with time-sensitive promotions to encourage quick action.

Leveraging Trends:

- **Stay Updated:** Monitor social media platforms and news for emerging trends.
- **Be Authentic:** Only engage with trends that align with your brand's values and tone.
- **Act Fast:** Trending topics have short lifespans, so speed is crucial for relevance.

10.3 INTEGRATING WHATSAPP INTO YOUR MARKETING FUNNEL

WhatsApp is more than a messaging app; it's a valuable tool for building relationships and driving conversions. With over 2 billion users globally, integrating WhatsApp into your marketing strategy can help you reach your audience more directly.

How to Use WhatsApp in Marketing:

1. **Set Up a Business Profile:** Use WhatsApp Business to create a professional profile with your logo, contact information, and a description of your offerings.
2. **Leverage Automated Messages:** Use quick replies, greetings, and away messages to ensure timely communication.
3. **Share Personalized Offers:** Send tailored discounts or recommendations based on customer preferences.
4. **Provide Customer Support:** Use WhatsApp to answer inquiries, resolve issues, and build trust.
5. **Incorporate into Campaigns:** Add WhatsApp as a contact option in ads, newsletters, and your website.

Benefits:

- High engagement rates.
- Instant communication.

- Enhanced customer satisfaction.

10.4 COMMON PITFALLS TO AVOID

Even experienced marketers encounter challenges. Awareness of common pitfalls can help you navigate around them.

Key Pitfalls:

1. **Neglecting Mobile Optimization:** Ensure ads, landing pages, and emails are mobile-friendly, as most users access content via their phones.
2. **Overlooking Audience Segmentation:** Avoid using one-size-fits-all messaging. Personalization improves engagement and conversion rates.
3. **Ignoring Analytics:** Regularly review performance metrics to understand what's working and where improvements are needed.
4. **Overloading on Features:** Keep your messaging clear and concise. Too many features or calls-to-action can overwhelm your audience.
5. **Focusing Only on New Customers:** Balance efforts between acquiring new customers and nurturing existing ones. Repeat customers often have higher lifetime value.

By implementing these advanced strategies and avoiding common mistakes, you can refine your marketing efforts, maximize ROI, and stay ahead in the competitive landscape.

Conclusion

Recap of Key Takeaways

Throughout this book, we've journeyed through the multifaceted world of digital marketing with a focus on Meta's platforms—Facebook, Instagram, and WhatsApp. Here are the pivotal lessons we've learned:

- **Understanding Meta**: We explored how Meta's platforms provide unparalleled reach and engagement opportunities, making them essential tools for any marketer.
- **Organic vs. Paid**: We distinguished between organic growth and paid advertising, emphasizing the strategic use of both to maximize visibility and engagement.
- **Ad Creation**: From simple boosted posts to complex campaigns in Ads Manager, we've covered how to craft ads that resonate with your audience.
- **Budgeting and Optimization**: We delved into the mechanics of ad budgets, bidding strategies, and how to measure success through key performance metrics.
- **Automation**: The potential of automated ads to scale your efforts was discussed, highlighting the balance between automation and manual oversight for optimal results.
- **Creative and Targeting**: Importance of quality content, precise audience targeting, and continuous testing to refine ad performance.
- **Analytics and Iteration**: The need for ongoing analysis and adjustment to keep campaigns effective in a dynamic digital environment.

Encouragement to Start Your Digital Marketing Journey

Embarking on digital marketing with Meta's platforms can seem daunting, but remember:

- **Start Small**: You don't need to launch massive campaigns right away. Begin with small, manageable steps, learning from each campaign to build your confidence and expertise.
- **Experiment**: Don't be afraid to try new strategies or creative ideas. The digital landscape rewards innovation and adaptation.
- **Learn from Mistakes**: Every marketer makes mistakes. Use

them as learning opportunities to refine your strategies.

- **Consistency Over Perfection**: Regular engagement with your audience is more effective than waiting for the "perfect" campaign. Consistency builds brand familiarity and trust.
- **Stay Curious**: Digital marketing is an ever-evolving field. Keep your curiosity alive to stay ahead of trends and changes.

Remember, each click, like, and share is a step forward in understanding your audience and growing your brand. Your journey in digital marketing is not just about promoting products or services; it's about building connections, creating value, and achieving growth.

Resources for Ongoing Learning

To ensure your digital marketing skills continue to grow, here are some resources:

- **Meta Blueprint**: Meta's own training platform offers free courses from basic to advanced levels on using their advertising tools effectively.
- **Online Courses**: Platforms like Coursera, Udemy, and LinkedIn Learning provide courses on digital marketing, SEO, analytics, and more.
- **Blogs and Newsletters**: Follow industry leaders like Moz, HubSpot, or Neil Patel for the latest insights and strategies in digital marketing.
- **Webinars and Workshops**: Many marketing agencies and tools providers host webinars that can offer practical advice and case studies.
- **Communities and Forums**: Engage with communities on Reddit, specialized FB Groups, or platforms like Stack Exchange for peer-to-peer learning and problem-solving.
- **Books and eBooks**: There's a wealth of knowledge in books by digital marketing experts. Keep an eye out for updated editions that reflect the latest trends.
- **Certifications**: Consider getting certified in areas like Google Ads or Analytics to add credibility to your skill set.
- **Conferences**: Even if virtual, conferences offer networking opportunities and insights from industry leaders.

- **Analytics Tools**: Tools like Google Analytics, SEMrush, or Ahrefs are not only for monitoring but also for learning about SEO, user behavior, and more.

The digital marketing landscape is vast and ever-changing. By committing to continuous learning and adaptation, you'll not only keep up but also lead in your marketing endeavors. Here's to your success in navigating and thriving within the digital realm with Meta's powerful advertising tools.

www.ingramcontent.com/pod-product-compliance
Lightning Source LLC
La Vergne TN
LVHW051751050326
832903LV00029B/2844